for
beginners

AI in Robotics for Beginners

Discover How Artificial Intelligence Powers Intelligent Robots and Automation

Printed in the United States of America

First Edition: 2025

This copyright page includes the necessary copyright notice, permissions request information, acknowledgments for the cover design, interior design, and editing, as well as the details of the first edition.

www.littlebiggiant.com

Introduction

The small robot on the table blinked blue eyes and reached for the pencil. Hands hovered above the wood. Alex's breath felt loud in the quiet workshop. The robot's arm stopped, then tilted, then gently nudged the pencil toward the edge. It was supposed to follow a fixed line on the floor. It was not supposed to think about a pencil.

"It moved on its own," someone whispered. "Why did it do that?" The words came out sharp and small. Confusion tasted like metal and solder. The teacher crossed the room with steady steps. "Take a breath," the teacher said. "It learned from the last run." Alex's stomach dropped. Learning sounded like magic now. Learning sounded like a choice.

Lights hummed. The robot clicked softly as if deciding whether to pick the pencil up or leave it. Outside, a delivery van rolled past. Inside, the robot turned its small head toward the sound, then back again. The moment stretched longer than it should have. A hand reached out, but did not touch. Curiosity and worry tangled in the same knot.

This is where the facts matter. Known fact: by 2019, about 2.7 million industrial robots were operating in factories around the world. Those robots handled repeated tasks like welding and packing. New kinds of robots use artificial intelligence to learn from examples and change what they do. That change is what makes a robot reach for a pencil instead of following a line. It is what puts choices into metal and code.

The room felt warmer and stranger at once. The teacher smiled, not with answers, but with the kind of patience that says there will be answers soon. "Understanding the rules helps," the teacher said. "So does asking better questions." Alex watched the robot's arm hover. The pencil teetered. No one touched it. The whole workshop waited as if the next move might teach something important — or cause a mistake that could not be taken back.

Who will decide what that robot learns next, and how will that choice matter when robots do more than repeat tasks?

Table of Contents

Chapter 1

Foundations of Robotics and AI

By the end of this chapter you will understand what a robot is, how its parts work together, the basic AI ideas behind robot behavior, and the main software tools builders use to bring robotic ideas to life.

What is a robot? Actuators, sensors, and embedded systems

A robot is a machine that can sense the world, make some kind of decision, and then act on that decision. It's not just a toy or a gadget—it's designed to interact with its surroundings in a purposeful way. At the heart of every robot are three kinds of parts that work together.

First, actuators. Actuators are what let a robot move. They turn electrical energy into motion. The most common kinds are motors, which spin wheels or joints, and servos, which move a joint to a precise angle. Some robots use more powerful actuators for lifting or moving heavy objects, but the idea is the same: energy becomes motion. Think of a simple two-wheeled robot; each wheel is driven by a motor, and the speed of each motor controls where the robot goes. Or picture a small robotic arm with several joints; each joint is moved by a servo to pick up a cup or place a block.

Second, sensors. Sensors give robots eyes, ears, and touch. They collect data about the world so the robot can respond. Common examples include light or color sensors that detect a line on the floor, bump sensors that feel a collision, and distance sensors that tell how far something is away. Many robots also use cameras, much like your eyes, to capture pictures. Other sensors like gyroscopes or accelerometers tell the robot how it's tilting or moving through space. All these inputs feed into the robot's "brain" to build a picture of what's happening around it.

Third, embedded systems. An embedded system is like a tiny computer built into the robot. It runs software that reads sensor data, makes decisions, and sends commands to the actuators. There are different levels of computing inside a robot. A small microcontroller can handle simple, fast tasks—like reading a switch and turning on a motor. A single-board computer, such as a small Raspberry Pi or similar device, can run more complex programs, handle camera processing, or manage more sensors at once. In practice, a robot often uses a combination: a microcontroller handles real-time sensor reading and motor control, while a more powerful onboard computer runs the AI software and higher-level planning.

How these parts fit together is easier to see with a few everyday examples. A tiny line-following robot uses a set of reflectance sensors to detect a black line on a white surface. The sensors feed data to the onboard computer, which compares what it sees to the line it's supposed to follow. Based on that comparison, the software sends commands to the two motors to steer left or right, keeping the robot on track. A small robotic arm on a tabletop robot uses a camera to locate a block, a servo to move a joint to the right angle, and a motor to close a gripper around the block. In both cases, sensors gather data, the embedded system runs a decision process, and actuators carry out the chosen action.

A useful way to think about it is to picture a simple loop: observe, understand, act. The robot looks around with its sensors, uses software to interpret the data, and then uses its motors or other actuators to respond. The loop repeats, often many times per second, so the robot can adapt as things change in the scene.

Two short micro-cases help bring this to life. Case one: a toy rover with wheels and bump sensors. When the bump sensor feels a collision, the embedded controller quickly stops the motors and reverses just enough to avoid getting stuck. Case two: a kitchen helper bot with a small arm. The camera and touch sensors help it locate a mug, the controller computes a safe path to pick it up, and the arm moves to grasp it without knocking over nearby objects. In both cases, you can see how actuators, sensors, and an embedded brain work in harmony.

Core AI concepts for robotics: agents, perception, and planning

Robots use a few basic AI ideas to act intelligently in real life. These ideas aren't fancy magic; they're practical models for how a machine can behave in a real environment.

Agents. An agent is anything that can observe the world, decide what to do next, and take actions to reach a goal. A robot is a classic example: its goal might be "move from here to there without hitting anything," or "pick up the mug and place it on the table." In simple terms, an agent has a job, looks around, makes a choice, and does something. Some robots are reactive, meaning they respond quickly to immediate inputs. Others are more deliberative, planning several steps ahead. Either way, the idea is the same: set a goal, sense what's around you, and act to move toward that goal.

Perception. Perception is about turning raw sensory data into useful information. It's not enough to "see" something; you need to understand what you're seeing. Perception includes recognizing lines and colors, counting objects, estimating distance, and identifying where objects are in space. The more the robot perceives accurately, the better its decisions will be. In practice, perception combines data from many sensors to reduce uncertainty. For example, a delivery robot might use a camera to read a doorway sign and a distance sensor to avoid obstacles, then fuse that information to decide the best path.

Planning. Once the robot has a sense of the world and a goal, it creates a plan—a sequence of actions that will lead from the current state to the goal. Planning answers questions like: Where should I go next? How can I get there without colliding with walls or people? How do I pick up an object and move it to another location? In simple terms, planning is the robot's roadmap for action. It can be as straightforward as "go straight, then turn left at the intersection" or as careful as "compute a safe path that avoids moving pedestrians." In many robots, planning happens in layers: a quick, local decision to avoid a bump, plus a longer-range plan to complete a task.

Two micro-cases illustrate these ideas. First, a housekeeping robot in a school hallway uses perception to identify where people and doors are.

It uses planning to choose a safe route that minimizes disruption, adapting as people move. Second, a toy robot with a gripper learns to pick up a ball. It perceives the ball's position, decides when to extend the arm, and plans a short sequence to grab and drop the ball into a box. In both cases, perception and planning work hand in hand to translate sensor data into useful action.

Overview of robot software stacks and development tools

Under the hood, a robot's brain runs in layers that sit on top of one another. The bottom layer is the hardware interface: drivers that talk to sensors and actuators. Above that sits the software layer that coordinates data flow and basic tasks, such as reading a camera frame or moving a motor at the right speed. Above that is a more flexible middle layer that handles messages, timing, and simple decision rules. At the top sits the application layer, where the robot's specific tasks live—navigation, manipulation, or interaction logic.

A popular way to structure this work is with a software stack that helps different parts talk to each other without being tangled. A widely used framework in robotics acts as a middleman for data: it publishes information from sensors as messages and subscribes to those messages for use by other parts of the system. This arrangement makes it easier to swap in new perception methods or new motion plans without rewriting everything from scratch. It's common to see people rely on this kind of framework to connect cameras, lidars, grippers, and planners with clean, modular code.

Languages and tools you'll see often include Python for quick, readable code and C++ for fast, efficient programs. If you work with more complex sensing or real-time control, you'll likely use both, switching to Python for wiring together components and C++ for the heavy-lifting parts that need speed. Version control, especially Git, becomes essential as soon as projects grow beyond a single file. For testing and validation, you'll hear about simulation environments where you can model robots and run your software without a real machine. Gazebo and Webots are two examples of popular sims that let you try routes and manipulation ideas safely. For actual hardware, you'll start with simple platforms and move up to more capable boards and sensors as you gain confidence.

Two brief micro-cases show how software stacks and tools come together. Case one: a student builds a small robot using a microcontroller for motor control and a camera for perception. They write Python scripts to grab images, run a tiny object detector, and publish motor commands through a simple message-passing system. The project runs in a light-weight simulator first, then on the real robot. Case two: a classroom project uses a ready-made robot kit with a programmable arm. The team uses a ROS-like system to connect the camera, gripper, and arm controller. They test with a river of small, repeatable tasks, logging results to refine their perception and planning steps.

A practical toolbox for budding builders

Tools you'll want as you start journeying into robotics include:

- A basic microcontroller or single-board computer for the "brain."

- A small set of actuators: motors for wheels or joints, and a simple gripper.

- A handful of sensors: a camera or light sensors, a distance sensor, and a bump sensor.

- A software stack that supports modular components and easy data sharing between sensors, planners, and actuators.

- A simple programming language that you enjoy, with Python and C++ as common choices.

- A version-control habit, like saving your work in a repository as you build.

Templates and quick-start checklists

- Component mapping template: List each sensor and actuator, note the data flow (sensor → brain → motor), and mark the expected response delay.

- Simple task plan template: Goal, current state, next action, safety constraints, the check to confirm completion.

- Safety and testing checklist: Power off before wiring, verify connections, test each sensor alone, test each motor alone, run a full dry-run in a simulator, then a slow real-world test with a clear safety zone.

Key Takeaway: A robot is built from three core ideas—movement (actuators), sensing (sensors), and smart control (an embedded brain). The AI ideas of agents, perception, and planning give robots the ability to act with purpose in the real world, guided by software stacks that keep hardware, software, and goals connected.

Coming up next, we dive into Sensors and Perception and learn how robots read their world through cameras, lasers, and touch, plus how to combine these signals into useful knowledge for safe and effective action.

Chapter 2

Sensors and Perception

You will learn the five sensors that most beginners start with: cameras, LIDAR, IMU, sonar, and tactile sensors. Each one gives you a different kind of information about the world, and together they help a robot see, sense, and move more reliably.

Step 1: Know what each sensor measures. A camera acts like two eyes for a machine. It captures light and turns it into pictures you can read on a screen. A LIDAR sends out light beams and measures how long they take to bounce back, building a distance map of the surroundings. An IMU, short for inertial measurement unit, watches acceleration and rotation to estimate how the robot is moving. Sonar uses sound waves to sense nearby objects, especially good for short distances and in cluttered rooms. Tactile sensors feel touch or pressure, giving a robot a sense of contact, grip, and texture. In practice, you'll often see cameras paired with IMUs or LIDAR to give both visual detail and precise motion information. For example, a tiny delivery robot might use a camera to recognize a doorway and an IMU to keep track of its tilt and speed as it travels over a curb.

Step 2: Understand what data looks like from each sensor. A camera produces a stream of images; you measure color or grayscale values at millions of points every second. LIDAR generates a 3D cloud of points that represent distances to objects; you get a map rather than a single number. An IMU returns numbers for acceleration in three axes and rotation rates, plus sometimes a magnetic heading. Sonar gives a distance reading from a single beam or multiple beams in a simple pattern. Tactile sensors deliver a contact value, often at many points on a gripper or pad. The key idea is that each sensor has its own strengths and weaknesses: cameras give rich detail but need light; LIDAR provides precise distance but can be bulky and costly; IMUs are great for motion but drift over time; sonar is simple and reliable up close; tactile sensors tell you what you touch.

Step 3: Keep sensors honest with simple checks. Every sensor benefits from a quick sanity check. If a camera image looks dark or blurry, you know lighting conditions are affecting vision. If the LIDAR map shows strange “spikes” in distance, something is reflecting beams incorrectly. If the IMU readings jump suddenly without movement, you’re likely seeing a sensor glitch or vibration. Regular checks help you catch problems early and keep your robot operating safely.

Step 4: Start with a basic sensor stack you can test together. A simple, practical pairing is a camera with an IMU. Use the camera to see the world and the IMU to tell you how the robot is moving as it follows a line or avoids a chair. If you add a tactile sensor to a gripper, you can tell when you have a good grip and adjust before dropping an object. The aim is to prove to yourself that multiple sensors work together to produce more reliable behavior than any one sensor alone.

Step 5: Build intuition with a two-mini-cases approach. Case A uses a camera and IMU on a small robot car. When you walk the car through a doorway, the camera detects the doorway's edge while the IMU tracks bank and tilt as the car navigates the threshold. Case B uses a camera, LIDAR, and tactile feedback on a simple robotic arm. The camera helps you see the object, LIDAR gives distance to the object, and the tactile sensor confirms when you've actually grabbed it. Notice how each sensor's data aligns to give a clearer picture of what's happening.

Step 6: Record practical limits you notice. Cameras struggle in low light or glare; LIDAR can miss things that are highly reflective or absorb light; IMUs drift slowly and need occasional correction using other sensors; sonar can be noisy in busy floors with many echoes; tactile sensors need careful placement to catch meaningful contact. By logging these limits, you'll know when to trust which data and when to switch to a different sensor fusion approach.

Signal Processing Basics and Multi-Sensor Fusion

You will dive into how to clean sensor data, merge information from several sensors, and keep your robot's understanding steady even when data looks noisy or incomplete.

Step 1: Learn the goal of signal processing. At a basic level, signal processing means cleaning up noise, filling in small gaps, and turning raw measurements into useful numbers you can act on. Think of it like polishing a rough stone so you can see the shape clearly. Noise can come from electrical interference, lighting flicker, or imperfect sensor hardware. The job is to separate the real signal—the true scene or motion—from the noise.

Step 2: Try simple filtering ideas. A quick, practical way to reduce noise is to average a few recent readings. For a camera, you might average a few frames to smooth sudden brightness changes; for a distance sensor, you can average several distance measurements before you decide how far away something is. The benefit is smoother, more stable data; the cost is a tiny delay, which you would tolerate in safe, non-high-speed tasks.

Step 3: Respect the time component. Sensor data arrives in time. If you ignore timing, you'll mix old information with new in confusing ways. When you compare an image frame with a distance reading, align them by their timestamps. If you can, keep a small log of recent measurements and their times so you can reconstruct what happened at any moment.

Step 4: Mix data from different sensors with a light touch. Multi-sensor fusion means using more than one sensor to form a better understanding.

Start with a simple idea: if both a camera and LIDAR say there's an obstacle at a certain distance, you can trust that reading more than if only one sensor says so. If the readings disagree, you use the sensor you trust more in that situation or you defer decision while you gather more data. The key is redundancy: multiple sources confirm the same reality, making the robot more reliable.

Step 5: Keep fusion practical and explainable. You don't need to build fancy math from scratch to begin. Start with straightforward rules: weigh each sensor by how confident you feel about it in the current scene, and update these weights over time as sensors prove themselves or fail. For learners, this approach is a powerful first step toward more formal methods later on.

Step 6: See how fusion helps in tricky environments. In a cluttered room, a camera might be blinded by shadows or glare, while LIDAR still gives you a rough map of obstacles. In a fast-moving robot, the IMU helps you keep track of quick rotations while camera data catches up. Fusion makes the robot more robust because it does not rely on just one sense. You get a fuller picture, even when one channel is weak.

Turning Sensor Data into Usable Features and Representations

You will transform raw sensor streams into things a robot can reason about and act on.

Step 1: Move from raw data to simple features. Features are bite-sized summaries of what the sensor sees. For a camera, features could be edges, corners, or textures; for a distance sensor, a feature could be "object distance within 1 meter." Turning raw images into edges or rough shapes is a practical first step. For distance data, turning the cloud into a surface or a silhouette helps planning and navigation.

Step 2: Build a compact scene representation. Don't store every pixel or every distance number. Keep a compact map or a simplified view of the environment. For beginners, that might mean a 2D occupancy map: a grid where each cell is either free space, occupied, or unknown. This representation is easy to reason about and quick to update as new sensor frames arrive.

Step 3: Match features across time and sensors. If you see a corner in one camera frame, search for the same corner in the next frame and in the LIDAR map. This matching gives you continuity: you can track how objects and the robot itself move, even as perspectives change. The more consistent your features are over time, the steadier your robot's understanding becomes.

Step 4: Use representation thoughtfully in tasks. If you're navigating, the occupancy map helps decide where you can go. If you're grasping, tactile features tell you when you've securely grabbed something. If you're avoiding obstacles, a combination of feature tracks and distance cues keeps you safe. Practice shows you which representations help most in a given job.

Step 5: Keep it simple at first, then layer in complexity. It's easy to want perfect models, but you'll learn faster by starting with clear, small features and a straightforward map. As you gain experience, you can add richer representations—like 3D maps or learned features from a neural network—one piece at a time.

Example 1: A small line-following robot uses a camera to see the line and an IMU to stay balanced as it moves. The camera produces a bright line on a dark floor; the IMU tells you if the robot tips sideways when it hits a bump. You filter the camera signal to reduce flicker and fuse it with the IMU's tilt reading to keep the robot on track, even on a rough surface. You record a smoother path and fewer slip-offs.

Example 2: A simple rover uses a camera and a short-range LIDAR to detect doors and avoid walls. The camera helps you recognize the door frames; the LIDAR confirms the distance to the wall before you steer away. You generate a tiny occupancy map from LIDAR and use camera cues to label features in that map. Results show up as safer navigation through a tight corridor with fewer near-misses.

Two short exercises you can try now

Exercise 1: Sensor inventory and sanity check (10 minutes)

- List every sensor on a test robot and what data it gives you.

- For each sensor, perform a quick test to see if data looks reasonable (e.g., camera frames show a scene, IMU values change when you tilt the robot, LIDAR distances drop as you approach a wall).

- Expected outcome: you can name the data type and identify a quick fault to check if data looks off.

Exercise 2: Simple data fusion sketch (15 minutes)

- Take camera data and IMU data during a straight push of the robot.

- Note where the camera sees a change in the scene and where the IMU shows a shift in tilt.

- Create a simple rule: if both sensors agree about movement, act on it; if they disagree, hold for the next frame.

- Expected outcome: you gain a feel for how fusion stabilizes motion understanding.

Exercise 3: Feature-to-representation practice (15 minutes)

- Pick one scene: a door, a chair, or a table edge.

- Identify a feature from the sensor data (edge in a camera, corner in a frame, a narrow distance band in LIDAR).

- Translate that feature into a simple map update (e.g., mark a wall's edge in a 2D map).

- Expected outcome: you can move from a raw signal to a usable map update.

Exercise 4: Quick test of multi-sensor reliability (20 minutes)

- Pair two sensors (camera + LIDAR or camera + IMU) on a simple path.

- Track a short segment of travel and record when sensors agree and when they don't.

- Expected outcome: you see how redundancy helps and you identify a scenario where one sensor might be unreliable.

Troubleshooting and quick fixes

- Problem: Data from one sensor seems noisy or inconsistent.

Quick fix: apply a light filter and check timing synchronization. If the problem persists, temporarily rely more on another sensor while you investigate hardware or lighting issues.

- Problem: Fusion feels unstable or biased toward one sensor.

Quick fix: rebalance trust based on recent performance. Give slightly more weight to the sensor with fewer contradictions in the current scene.

- Problem: Features fail to appear in the representation.

Quick fix: choose simpler features first (edges or corners) and ensure the feature extraction aligns with the sensor data. If needed, reduce the resolution to stabilize detection.

- Problem: Delays in representation update slow down decisions.

Quick fix: reduce the number of steps in the processing chain, or process data in smaller chunks with a short, fixed delay that you can tolerate safely.

Templates and tools you can copy

- Sensor Catalog Template

Sensor name:

Data type (e.g., color image, depth, acceleration):

Typical rate:

Strengths:

Weaknesses:

Quick diagnostic checks:

- Simple Fusion Checklist

[ ] Are sensor times aligned?

[ ] Do we have a basic, robust feature for each sensor?

[ ] Is the fusion rule simple and interpretable?

[ ] Do we have a fallback plan if one sensor fails?

[ ] Have we tested in a low-risk environment first?

- Feature-to-Map Mapping Template

Feature observed:

Sensor source:

Map update decision:

Confidence level:

Next action:

Key Takeaway: When you mix different senses, you get a clearer, steadier view of the world than any single sensor can give you alone.

Coming up next Subtittle: Computer Vision for Robots

1) Image processing essentials: filtering, edges, and segmentation,

2) Object detection and recognition with classical and deep methods,

3) Depth sensing, stereo vision, and scene understanding

Transition: In the next chapter, you'll learn how to turn those color images and depth cues into the kinds of decisions that let robots recognize objects, estimate where they are in space, and plan safe, efficient paths. You'll explore practical image techniques, simple detection methods, and how depth adds meaning to what the robot "sees."

Chapter 3

Computer Vision for Robots

1) Image processing essentials: filtering, edges, and segmentation

You start with a camera's raw picture, and your goal is to make patterns in that picture useful for your robot. The first tool is filtering, or filtering out the noise that quietly hides every detail. Think of smoothing as steady rain on a window: the glass fogs a little, but you still see the big shapes clearly.

In robots, a common approach is a gentle blur called Gaussian smoothing. It reduces tiny specks and random brightness bumps that would otherwise confuse later steps. The result is a cleaner image where real objects stand out more clearly.

After you've reduced noise, you want to find the boundaries where one thing ends and another begins. These boundaries are called edges. Edges show where colors change, where a table meets the floor, or where a ball stands out from a dark background. Edge detection spots those sharp changes in brightness or color, and it highlights the lines that define shapes. You don't need every edge to be perfect to be useful; you just need enough signal to tell what is what. A common idea is to measure how quickly brightness changes from one pixel to the next, and then connect those rapid changes into curves that outline objects.

Segmentation is the next step: grouping parts of the image into meaningful chunks, like "this is the ball," "this is the floor," "this is the wall." You can keep things simple with thresholding—saying "everything lighter than this is background, everything darker is object." But thresholds can be fussy; lighting can change the whole game. A more flexible approach groups similar pixels by several features, such as color and brightness, or even uses tiny patterns to decide whether two neighboring pixels belong to the same object. The aim is to turn a flat picture into a map of pieces you can act on.

When segmentation succeeds, your robot can locate objects, estimate their sizes, and decide where to move or reach.

Three things to keep in mind as you practice: lighting matters, noise matters, and scale matters. If you shoot in a bright room, walls might wash out fine edges; in a dim room, you'll need stronger filtering or different thresholds. If there's a lot of tiny texture, your segmentation might split one object into many pieces; you can fix this by adjusting the balance between color and brightness, or by using a broader feature set. And never forget to test with real scenes: a kitchen, a classroom, or a toy-strewn desk are great laboratories for seeing how your image processing holds up under everyday variation.

Two quick examples to see the ideas in action: first, a small robot cleaner looks at a messy floor and uses smoothing to reduce speckles from dust. Then edge detection helps it distinguish the edge of a rug from the tile, so it doesn't stumble or slide off. The second example involves sorting toys: a camera captures a mixed pile of red and blue blocks. A simple color threshold helps separate the red blocks from the blue ones, while a quick segmentation step groups same-colored pixels into blobs that you can count or pick up. If the lighting changes or the blocks touch, you adjust by widening the color range a touch and letting the segmentation group nearby pixels more generously.

Practical tips to keep you moving: start with a bright, uncluttered scene to learn the basics, then slowly introduce noise and variation to see what breaks first. Test one step at a time—first filtering, then edge detection, then segmentation—so you know exactly where things go right or wrong. If you get inconsistent results, check your camera exposure and white balance, then revisit your thresholds. And keep a simple visual log: save before and after pictures for each stage so you can compare how each step changes the view your robot uses to decide what to do.

2) Object detection and recognition with classical and deep methods

Detection and recognition are two stances your robot uses for seeing. Detection asks, “Is there something interesting here?” and where is it? Recognition asks, “What is this thing?” and can include identifying its category or name. In classic, hands-on robotics, people used carefully designed features—patterns the computer could recognize reliably—to find objects. These are called hand-crafted features. You might hear about Haar-like features, which look for simple patterns of light and dark, or HOG (Histogram of Oriented Gradients), which captures the shape of a person or an object by how edges align. These methods work well in controlled scenes, especially when you can tell the robot exactly what to expect.

In recent years, deep learning brought a bigger shift. Neural networks can learn from lots of pictures to spot many kinds of objects, even when the scenes are messy or surprising. In a typical setup, you feed the robot hundreds or thousands of labeled images, showing the objects you care about in many poses, colors, and lighting. The network learns to map the pixels to object identities and locations. The result is powerful: a robot can detect several kinds of objects in real time, drawing bounding boxes around them and labeling what they are. The most popular families of methods are end-to-end detectors that predict both where an object is and what it is in one pass. These methods make mistakes too—occlusion, partial views, or objects that look like others can confuse them—but with good training data and a careful setup, they're incredibly effective.

Two short scenarios illustrate the idea. In a home classroom, a small assistant robot uses a classical detector to find a mug and a book on a desk. The detector looks for familiar shapes and colors, marks their boxes, and then sends a signal to pick up the mug if it's within reach. In a toy factory, another robot uses a deep detector to spot multiple kinds of parts on a belt—cubes, cylinders, and caps—while the camera moves quickly. The detector must be fast and stable, so engineers often trade a little speed for more reliable recognition, or they use a lighter, more efficient model for real-time operation.

A few practical notes to keep in mind as you practice: begin with simple, well-lit scenes and a limited set of objects. Use a pre-trained detector when you're just learning, but don't rely on it forever—your robot will need to understand new objects as your tasks grow. Balance the data you train on: if most of your images show objects from one angle, the detector may fail when the angle shifts. Also, keep an eye on background clutter. A busy scene can fool even a good detector if the background shares similar colors or shapes with the target. To improve robustness, you can augment your training with variations—flip images, adjust brightness, simulate shadows—so the detector learns to handle real-world variability.

Two concise examples help bring this to life. First, a kid-friendly robot at a maker space learns to identify three items—cup, ball, and marker—using a mix of classical features and a lightweight neural model. It locates each item, estimates its position, and then hands the item to the user when asked. Second, imagine a small warehouse robot equipped with a deep detector that recognizes a box, a label, and a barcode. It uses these cues not only to see the object but also to confirm its identity before guiding a gripper to pick it up. In both cases, detection provides a map of where things are, while recognition tells you what those things are, guiding the robot's next move.

If you run into trouble, here are quick fixes. If detections flicker or miss items, you might need more lighting, a different camera angle, or a broader training set that covers those edge cases. If a detector confuses two similar objects, consider adding a secondary, simpler classifier that looks for a distinguishing cue—like a distinctive color patch or a unique texture. For deep methods, ensure your model isn't overfitting to a small dataset; validate on new images that weren't seen during training. Remember, you can often get strong results by combining methods: use a fast, classical detector to get candidate objects and then refine with a deeper model for final labels.

Two micro-cases to practice with right away: one, a personal robot friend in a room with several household items learns to detect a cup, a book, and a phone. It tracks their positions as you move, and it responds when you point at one, saying its name aloud. Two, a classroom robot sorts colored blocks by shape using a simple recognition cue (for example, detecting circles vs. squares) and then places each block into the corresponding colored bin. The goal in each case is not perfection but consistent, observable behavior you can build on as you experiment further.

3) Depth sensing, stereo vision, and scene understanding

Depth adds a third dimension to your robot's view: how far away things are. With depth, a robot can judge distances, avoid collisions, and plan where to move or reach. There are different paths to depth. Stereo vision uses two cameras placed a short distance apart, like human eyes. Each camera sees the scene from a slightly different angle, and the computer compares the two views to estimate how far each point lies from the cameras. The differences in what each eye sees are called disparities, and from those disparities you build a depth map. It's a clever trick that works best when the scene contains textured surfaces that provide clear correspondences between the two views.

Besides stereo, many depth sensors are active. They project a pattern of light or pulses and measure the time it takes for that light to bounce back. Time-of-flight sensors and structured-light sensors fall into this category. The result is a depth map that shows the distance to every pixel in the image, which your robot can turn into a three-dimensional understanding of the scene. Depth sensing helps with precise reaching and navigation, especially when the robot needs to avoid obstacles that lie on the floor or at head height.

Scene understanding blends color, texture, and depth to create a mental model of what the robot is looking at. It's about recognizing surfaces (like walls, floors, and tables), identifying objects, and figuring out how they relate to each other in space. With depth information, you can tell not just that a block is present, but that it sits on the table in front of you, or that a chair is next to a desk and blocking a path. Scene understanding is what allows a robot to plan a safe path, decide where to grasp an object, and even predict what might happen next in a scene where people are moving.

Two practical examples make depth and scene understanding concrete. First, a toy robot vacuum uses depth cues to avoid stepping off a raised edge or getting stuck on a rug with a soft, uneven surface. It creates a rough map of the room, then uses that map to navigate efficiently while avoiding collisions. Second, a helper robot in a kitchen uses stereo vision to estimate the distance to a mug on a countertop. It checks depth to ensure its gripper aligns properly with the mug's handle, then adjusts its approach to pick it up safely without tipping the mug.

There are common challenges to remember. Reflective surfaces—like a shiny countertop or a glass door—can confuse depth sensors because the projected patterns bounce in unexpected ways. Low-texture areas can also be hard for stereo cameras; without good texture, it's tough to match points between the two views. To counter these issues, you combine cues: use depth data together with color and edge information, add redundancy by using multiple sensors when possible, and keep expectations modest in tricky environments. The goal is not to achieve perfect depth everywhere but to have reliable depth where it matters for your robot's tasks.

Two examples to illustrate how depth and scene understanding support action: in a pico-robot kitchen, depth helps the robot place a cup down gently without tipping it, because it knows exactly how far away the cup is and how high the shelf is. In a small classroom, a robot assistant uses depth to navigate around desks and identify a student's hand reaching for a marker, so it can gently pass the marker without colliding with someone's elbow. These moments show how depth and scene understanding turn flat images into actionable knowledge about the real world.

Key Takeaway: Images become meaningful when you add edges, segments, objects, and depth. By smoothing noise, outlining boundaries, recognizing what things are, and measuring how far they are, your robot moves from seeing to understanding.

Coming up next: Localization and Mapping. You'll build on what you've learned by learning how robots figure out where they are in the world and how they create maps of their surroundings. You'll explore odometry, pose estimates, and the basics of SLAM, so your robot can navigate with confidence and keep its map accurate as the world changes around it.

Chapter 4

Localization and Mapping

By the end of this chapter you will understand how a robot keeps track of its own position and builds a map of its surroundings using three core ideas: odometry and pose estimation, SLAM with map representations and probabilistic thinking, and loop closure to keep maps accurate.

Odometry and Pose Estimation Fundamentals

You start with odometry. Odometry is how you estimate movement by watching how your wheels or joints turn. If you have wheel encoders, you can count how many times a wheel spins and from that guess how far you've moved. If your robot has joints, you can track the rotation of those joints to see how the arm or chassis has shifted. Odometry is fast and simple, but it isn't perfect. Slippery floors, bumps, or a wheel that spins without grabbing the ground can make the estimate slide off in the wrong direction.

Think of pose estimation as your best guess of where you are in space. Pose means where you are and which way you're facing. To improve this guess, you mix odometry with other signals from the robot. If you have an inertial sensor, like an accelerometer or gyroscope, you get clues about rotation and motion that help correct the drift from odometry alone. If you have a camera or a distance sensor, those clues can tell you, "I'm a bit to the left of where the wheel turns say I should be."

In practice, you combine sources to form a more reliable estimate of position and orientation over time. A common pattern is to update your pose estimate as you move, then gently adjust it when a stronger sensor tells you a slightly different story. I've learned from hands-on testing that keeping the sensors well aligned and calibrated matters a lot. If a sensor is off by a small amount, it can tilt your entire map out of true, especially after you've walked a long path.

A simple, concrete example helps. Imagine a small rover moving down a straight hallway. Odometry tells you "I moved forward this much," but if the floor is slick, the wheel might spin a little and your odometry says you've gone farther than you really have. If you also measure a slight turn with the gyroscope, you can notice that the straight path isn't perfect and you can correct your straight-line assumption. The result is a pose estimate that stays reasonable longer, even when the floor isn't perfect. Another quick example: a robot with a forward-facing camera sees a familiar corner it saw earlier. The camera's view can help you realize you're a bit off from where your wheel counts say you should be, so you nudge your pose back toward the truth.

Key ideas to carry forward:

- Odometry gives you step-by-step movement; it's fast but biased by wheel slip, slippage, and small errors.

- Pose estimation blends multiple signals to improve accuracy over time.

- Regular calibration and sensor alignment pay off because even small misalignments ripple into bigger map errors later.

SLAM Principles, Map Representations, and Probabilistic Frameworks

SLAM stands for simultaneous localization and mapping. The core idea is to figure out where you are (localization) while you're building a map of the world around you (mapping—what the robot sees and where it is in relation to those things). You do not need to know the map in advance; the robot learns it as it moves. This is powerful because it lets a robot explore new places without a pre-made blueprint.

There are a few ways to represent the map, and each has its own tricks. One common approach is an occupancy grid. In an occupancy grid, the space is divided into small cells, and each cell has a probability that it is occupied by something (like a wall or obstacle). When your sensors see walls and obstacles, you update these cells to reflect higher or lower chances of being blocked. Another approach uses features or landmarks: places the robot recognizes by distinctive patterns, corners, or textures. A third option uses a point cloud or a 3D map, which helps in environments with height differences or stairs.

Behind the scenes, SLAM often relies on probabilistic thinking. Sensors aren't perfect, and your movements aren't exact. A probabilistic approach keeps track of what could be true, given all the evidence you've collected. You don't get a single point of truth; you get a distribution of possibilities, and you update that distribution as you sense more.

Two familiar faces in this space are the Kalman filter family and particle filters. A Kalman filter is a tidy, fast way to fuse ideas when you believe errors follow a smooth, known pattern. It works well when your motion and sensing models are fairly linear and the noise is roughly Gaussian. A particle filter takes a different path: it represents many possible states at once by sampling lots of tiny "particles" through space. Each particle carries a guess of where the robot could be, and sensors give each guess a score. The best guesses get more weight, and over time you converge toward the most plausible location and map. You don't need to understand all the math to use the idea: think of it as trying out many possible paths and keeping the ones that fit the world you see.

A practical map also needs to stay useful as you move. The map must be update-friendly—new lines of walls, new doors, and changes in the scene should slide into your representation without breaking what you already know. That's where probabilistic thinking shines: it naturally accommodates new information and shifts confidence up or down in different parts of the map.

Two short micro-cases show how this works. Case one is a cleaning robot moving from a kitchen into a dining area. It starts by sketching a rough grid: "I think the wall is roughly here," based on the laser or depth camera. As it explores the dining room, it sees more features and revises its grid: walls become clearer, furniture is placed on the map, and the robot's sense of its own location tightens. Case two is a delivery bot moving through a corridor with doors along the side. It relies on a feature-based map: door frames, corner features, and floor texture. When lighting changes or a door is opened, the robot updates its expectations and keeps the map consistent by adjusting the probable locations of those landmarks.

Key ideas to carry forward:

- SLAM lets you localize while mapping, without a prior map.

- Map representations can be grids, features, or 3D points; choose what matches your environment.

- Probabilistic frameworks handle uncertainty and update maps as new data arrives.

- Sensor fusion and careful data association (deciding which feature in the current observation corresponds to which feature in the map) are essential for reliability.

Loop Closure, Map Optimization, and Dealing with Drift

As you move, your estimates accumulate error. The longer you walk, the more drift you can build up—your internal map may slowly drift away from the real world. Loop closure is the moment you realize you've been in a location before. Maybe you turned a corner and saw the same door you passed earlier. When that happens, you have a chance to tie together two parts of your map that looked different before, and you can correct errors that have crept in.

Loop closure is like solving a puzzle where you now know that two separate sections of the map actually connect. Detecting a loop relies on recognizing places that look familiar: a distinctive corner, a doorway, or a unique arrangement of objects. Once you confirm a loop, you re-balance the entire map to bring the old and new observations into alignment. Think of it as a global adjustment: if you find out you were walking a little to the left all along, you shift that part of the map to match where you truly were.

Map optimization goes hand-in-hand with loop closure. After you discover a loop, you don't just fix a single spot; you adjust many parts of the map to keep everything consistent. In computer terms, this is often done with a graph: nodes represent robot poses or landmarks, and edges represent constraints from sensor measurements. The optimization process looks for the most plausible arrangement of nodes that respects all those constraints. It's a safety net: when new information contradicts the old, the system gently tilts the map back toward what the world is actually showing you.

Drift is the natural leftover error you can't completely erase. It's the reason loop closures matter. Without loops, drift grows without bound and your map becomes less and less reliable. With loops, drift can be corrected, keeping your map stable even after long journeys through complex spaces. I've learned that the best practice is to design paths or exploration patterns that encourage revisiting familiar places. It doesn't have to be deliberate—just moving in loops or retracing routes helps the system find those natural loop closures.

Two micro-cases illustrate loop closure and drift correction. Case one: a robot vacuum maps a living room, then returns to its charging dock. If the dock location is a bit off from the original estimate, loop closure helps bring the two areas together and fix the drift. Case two: a drone surveys a warehouse and later re-enters the same aisle from a different angle. Detecting the earlier shelves in the new view allows the system to align the two views, making the map more accurate and saving the drone from getting lost in the same space twice.

Key ideas to carry forward:

- Drift happens when estimates slowly go off target; drift worsens with longer paths and more complex motion.

- Loop closure recognizes previously seen places to force a consistent map.

- Graph-based optimization adjusts multiple poses and landmarks to fit all observations together.

- Real-world reliability improves when you plan routes that give the system opportunities to re-observe known places.

Key Takeaway: You build reliable maps by combining steady movement estimates with sensor fusion, recognize when you've revisited places to correct drift, and use global adjustments to keep your map aligned with the real world.

Coming up next: Motion Planning and Pathfinding

In motion planning you'll learn how a robot uses its map to decide where to go, how to avoid obstacles, and how to plan smooth paths that respect physical limits. You'll explore configuration spaces, simple and smart planners, and how to shape trajectories so a robot can move safely and efficiently through real spaces. This next chapter will show you how to turn a map into action, step by step.

Chapter 5

Motion Planning and Pathfinding

By the end of this chapter, you will understand how robots plan moves in space, choose planning methods, and turn a rough path into a smooth motion that respects how fast and how turning is allowed.

Configuration spaces and obstacle modeling

Think of a robot as a traveler that can be in many different places and, for some robots, facing different directions. A simple robot might only need x and y coordinates, but a real robot can also need to know its orientation or the angles of its joints. The collection of all those possibilities is called the configuration space. Each point in this space represents one exact pose of the robot—the exact way it sits or points in the world. Obstacles in the real world are things the robot cannot touch. In the configuration space, those obstacles become shapes as well: every position that would cause a collision is marked as blocked.

To make this easier to manage, you often grow the obstacles a bit. If your robot is a circle with a fixed radius, you can "inflate" each obstacle by that radius. This way, you only need to check whether the robot's center point lands inside a grown obstacle, rather than calculating every possible touch. With that change, the free space is the set of all configurations where the robot doesn't touch anything. Planning a path means tracing a line through the free space from the start pose to the goal pose without stepping into the blocked areas.

When you picture a tiny cleaning robot in a kitchen, the table legs, chair legs, walls, and the kitchen island all become inflated shapes in the configuration space. The robot's job is to move from its starting pose to the doorway without ever crossing into those inflated shapes. This way, the problem feels simpler: you plan a route that stays in the safe zone, not a route through every single obstacle in the room.

Step 1: Decide what the robot must know. List the coordinates or angles that describe the robot's pose.

Step 2: Draw the obstacles in the real world as expanded shapes in the configuration space.

Step 3: Mark the safe, or free, areas where the robot can move without hitting anything.

Step 4: Use the free space as the map for choosing a path from start to goal, keeping you in safe territory.

A quick micro-case: A small warehouse robot that moves on a flat floor. It needs x, y, and a turning angle. Inflate the shelves a little, and you get a clear free region around each shelf. The robot can now plan a route by staying in the open spaces between inflated shelves instead of trying to weave through every edge of every obstacle.

Sampling- and graph-based planners: RRT, PRM, A*, Dijkstra

When the free space is complex—lots of nooks, tight passages, and many obstacles—you don't always draw a perfect line by hand. You use planners. There are two broad families: sampling-based planners and graph-based planners. Each has strengths in different situations.

RRT, or Rapidly-exploring Random Tree, is a sampling-based method designed to explore space quickly. It grows a tree by repeatedly picking a random point in the configuration space and connecting it to the closest point already in the tree, as long as the connection doesn't hit an obstacle. Over time, the tree spreads out and reaches the goal if there is a feasible route. RRT is great for finding paths fast in cluttered spaces, especially when you don't need the perfect shortest path.

PRM, or Probabilistic Roadmap, is another sampling-based approach but works a bit differently. It samples many random points in the free space and then connects nearby samples to form a network, or roadmap. Once the roadmap exists, you can run a standard graph search to find a path from start to goal. PRM shines when you'll reuse the same space multiple times. You build the roadmap once and solve many queries quickly.

A *and Dijkstra are graph-based search methods that work on a predefined network, grid, or roadmap. Dijkstra always finds the shortest path on a fixed graph, while A* adds a smart guess—the heuristic—to steer the search toward the goal more quickly. Heuristics are simple rules like "how far is my current point from the goal?" A* tends to be faster in practice because it prioritizes promising routes.

Step 1: Pick a planner type (sampling-based or graph-based) based on your space and how fast you need an answer.

Step 2: If using RRT, start with a random sampling process and grow a tree toward the goal while avoiding inflated obstacles.

Step 3: If using PRM, build a network by connecting nearby samples that are collision-free, then search the network for a path.

Step 4: If using A* or Dijkstra, lay out a graph that represents safe connections and run the search from start to goal.

Step 5: Test the result in the real or simulated world, adjust the model if paths skim obstacles or look impractical in tight spaces.

Two micro-cases help you see these ideas in action. Case one: a robot under time pressure must navigate a factory floor with many machines. RRT can quickly give you a feasible route around machines. Case two: a home helper robot revisits the same kitchen every morning. Build a PRM once, then reuse it to plan different trips between pantry, fridge, and sink. For both, you measure success by how reliably the path avoids obstacles and how long it takes to compute.

A note on choosing between methods. If you need a fast answer in a crowded space, sampling methods often win on speed. If you'll run many queries in the same area, a pre-built graph or roadmap can save time later. If you want a guaranteed best path on a simple grid, a well-tuned A* search can be the most predictable choice. Each method has trade-offs in speed, optimality, and memory use, so you often combine ideas for the best result.

Step 1: Decide what kind of space you're dealing with (dense with obstacles or open with few barriers).

Step 2: Choose a planner that fits your time and accuracy needs.

Step 3: Run the planner and examine the path for practicality—does it weave through tight corners or hug obstacles too closely?

Step 4: If the path isn't good enough, adjust the planning method, tweak the obstacle model, or add more samples to improve reliability.

A second micro-case shows the difference. In a hallway with a few people moving around, an RRT might produce a quick path that detours around people. In a warehouse with many shelves and repeated routes, PRM can create a robust network of possible paths that you can reuse each day.

Trajectory generation, smoothing, and kinodynamic constraints

Finding a route in space is not enough if the robot can't follow it smoothly. You need to turn a path into a motion plan: a path that also respects time, speed, and how the robot can accelerate or turn. This is called trajectory generation, and it works hand-in-hand with the robot's physical limits.

First, you take the path through space and parameterize it with time. You decide how fast the robot should move along each section, making sure it doesn't have to stop suddenly or whip around a corner. Then you generate a trajectory, which is the path plus a schedule: a sequence of positions with associated times.

Next comes smoothing. Real-world movement is not a stiff line; it should be gentle. You can smooth a path by using simple curves or splines, which turn sharp corners into gradual bends. The goal is to keep the path visually and physically pleasant while staying in safe zones.

Kinodynamic constraints are the rules your robot must follow, derived from its physics. They include maximum speed, maximum acceleration, and sometimes the limit on how quickly it can change direction (turning rate). For many robots, especially wheeled ones, you can't move sideways or instantly jump to a new orientation. The trajectory must respect those limits; otherwise, the robot might slide into an obstacle or tip over in a sharp turn.

To check feasibility, verify that every point along the trajectory stays within the free space you defined earlier and that velocity and acceleration stay within safe bounds. If anything looks unsafe, you adjust the timing, reduce speed in tricky sections, or nudge the path to be smoother. In dynamic environments, you may replan the trajectory on the fly as new information comes in—still keeping within the same kinodynamic rules.

Two quick examples help illustrate this. Example one: a small ground robot follows a planned path through a cluttered living room. You start with a grid-like route, then smooth it with a gentle curve so the robot doesn't need to stop at every corner. You check that the speed is not too high for the sharp turns, and you adjust if a chair leg becomes too close as the robot moves. Example two: a robotic arm moving between two poses along a straight line around a few other objects. You parameterize the arm's joints so the end effector moves smoothly, ensuring each joint stays within its limits and the motion feels natural and precise.

A practical note on reactivity. If a sudden obstacle appears or a moving person crosses the path, you may pause, re-sample, or replan the trajectory quickly. The most robust systems blend fast re-planning with a safe default trajectory so the robot can continue moving smoothly even when things change.

Step 1: Take your space path and assign times to points along it.

Step 2: Generate a smooth trajectory that respects max speed and max acceleration at every point.

Step 3: Apply smoothing techniques to remove sharp corners while keeping the path safe.

Step 4: Check kinodynamic constraints for every segment, adjusting speed or curvature as needed.

Step 5: Validate the trajectory by making sure it stays in free space throughout its run and that the timing feels natural for the robot's motors.

Step 6: If needed, replan or tweak the trajectory to account for new information or tighter spaces.

Two micro-cases for trajectory work. Case A: a ground robot speeding down a corridor with a few turns. Start with a rough path along the center of the corridor, then slow a little before each bend and smooth the segment to avoid jerky moves. The result is steady progress with safe clearance. Case B: a robotic arm delivering a tool at a workstation. The path should stay within joint limits and move with gentle acceleration so the tool arrives exactly when needed without overshoot.

Key Takeaway: You turn rough routes into safe, smooth, clocked motions by understanding the configuration space, choosing a planning method that fits the space, and shaping the path into a time-controlled trajectory that respects the robot's limits.

Coming up next: Control Systems and Navigation

In the next chapter, you will explore open-loop versus closed-loop control and the basics of PID genetics in motion. You will also see how model predictive control and adaptive methods offer smarter ways to guide robots, and you will learn how perception and control fit together to keep autonomous navigation reliable even in changing environments. This practical pairing of planning and control is what lets robots move with purpose instead of just drifting.

Chapter 6

Control Systems and Navigation

You will understand how to choose and apply control methods to keep a robot on its intended path, from simple open-loop setups to smart, perception-aware navigation.

Open-loop vs closed-loop control and PID fundamentals

Open-loop control is when you tell a robot to do something without watching what it actually did. It's like telling a friend to walk a straight line for 10 steps and hoping they stay on course, no matter what happens along the way. Closed-loop control, by contrast, watches what the robot is doing and uses feedback to correct its actions. If the robot veers off track, the controller nudges it back toward the target. This feedback is essential when the world isn't perfect—slippery floors, small bumps, or wheel slip can throw a robot off its path. Closed-loop control is the backbone of reliable navigation.

A simple, practical way to start is with a proportional controller, or a P controller. The idea is straightforward: if the robot's current position or orientation is off from the target, apply a correction that is proportional to that error. The bigger the error, the bigger the correction. This seems obvious, but in real life you'll quickly see that a pure proportional approach can overshoot or settle with a steady, tiny error if nothing else moderates it.

Now add a little memory and damping with a proportional-integral-derivative, or PID, controller. The P part reacts to the present error, the I part looks at accumulated past error to cancel steady drift, and the D part predicts future error by watching how quickly the error is changing. You don't need fancy math to start; you can tune each piece by listening to the robot and watching its behavior on a simple course.

Think through two concrete cases. Case one, a line-following robot on a narrow track. The line represents the goal, and your error is how far the robot's sensor line is from center. A modest P gain can keep the robot steady, but if the robot tends to sway back and forth, you'll add a small D term to damp the motion. If the robot slowly drifts away as it travels, you'll introduce a bit of I to remove that bias over time. Case two, a small rover moving on a rough surface. Small bumps disturb the motion, and the D term helps suppress rapid changes that would make the rover overshoot or jitter. The I term helps when the terrain causes a slow, persistent offset from the target.

Three practical steps guide you through this, each with a clear rationale:

Step 1: Define your error. Decide what the target state is and how you will measure how far you are from it. The simpler your environment, the easier this is to quantify. Rationale: Clear error signals are the fuel for feedback, and without a reliable error estimate you can't correct course.

Step 2: Start with a small proportional gain. Observe the response. Rationale: A small P gain gives you a stable baseline and helps you see how the system reacts without whipping the robot into oscillations.

Step 3: Add a touch of derivative or integral as needed. Observe again, adjusting slowly. Rationale: D smooths out fast swings; I removes slow drift. Each addition changes the feel of the navigation, so add only what you need.

Two short examples to bring this to life. Example A is a line-following robot. The robot uses a sensor strip to detect its distance from a line. With a small P gain, it stays roughly in line but wanders a bit. Add D to damp the swing as it corrects, and you see smoother steering. If you notice the robot gradually drifts away from the line, introduce a little I to compensate for that bias.

Example B is a small drone keeping altitude. When gusts lift or push the drone, the P term pushes back toward the target height, the D term dampens the immediate response to gusts, and the I term helps remove a tiny residual height error after the gust passes.

What can go wrong, and how to fix it quickly. If the robot starts to overshoot or oscillate, reduce the P gain or add a bit more damping with D. If it's slow to respond or never reaches the target, increase P slightly, but watch out for new oscillations. If there's a steady bias, introduce I to eliminate the bias over time. In practical terms, tuning is about making the robot feel "in control" rather than "always chasing the target."

Advanced controllers: model predictive control and adaptive methods

Model Predictive Control, or MPC, is one of the smarter ways to steer a robot when the world is more complicated. Imagine you could see a few seconds into the future and make a plan that keeps you on course while avoiding obstacles and staying within the robot's limits. MPC does exactly that, but with a built-in model of how the robot moves. It predicts what will happen if you take a sequence of actions, then chooses the best first action, updates the plan, and repeats. The horizon—how far into the future it looks—can be short for a small robot or longer for a vehicle with more computation. MPC handles constraints naturally: speed limits, turning radii, and obstacles all become part of the planning picture.

An adaptive approach is a different kind of smart. Adaptive controllers adjust their own parameters as the robot experiences different conditions. If you pick up a payload on a robot arm, the dynamics change; an adaptive controller notices the change and adjusts gains on the fly. The goal is to keep performance steady even when the robot's real-world dynamics shift.

Two illustrative applications help you see how these tools fit into practice. First, an automated ground vehicle on a loop with occasional obstacles.

A basic MPC can plan a safe path that respects speed limits and keeps a comfortable distance from walls or other cars. It continuously re-plans as new sensor data arrives, so a sudden obstacle is handled smoothly. Second, a robotic arm lifting objects of different weights. A controller that adapts its gains as the payload changes will keep the arm moving with steadier speed and less wobble, even if the weight shifts from test to test.

Three steps to get oriented with these advanced methods:

Step 1: Build a simple model and a horizon. Create a basic guess of how your robot moves and how long you want to look ahead before acting. Rationale: Even a small model helps you predict what happens next, which is the essence of predictive control.

Step 2: Add constraints and a cost measure. Decide what counts as "good" in your task: staying on a path, not exceeding speed, avoiding obstacles. Rationale: The plan should optimize safety and efficiency, not just reach a target.

Step 3: Implement a rolling update. After taking the first action, recompute the plan with new sensor data. Rationale: Real-world conditions change, and a rolling update keeps the plan relevant.

Two quick micro-cases show the idea. Micro-case 1 uses MPC for a tiny autonomous delivery vehicle navigating a curb-lined street. The controller forecasts several seconds of motion, respects a speed limit, and avoids parked cars, adjusting as pedestrians appear. Micro-case 2 uses an adaptive controller on a robotic arm that lifts objects from a conveyor at different weights. The system detects a shift in dynamics as the weight changes, and the gains adjust so the arm moves smoothly again without overshoot.

Integrating perception with control for robust autonomous navigation

Perception is how the robot sees the world. It feeds the control system with measurements, estimates where it is, and what obstacles lie ahead. The core idea is to connect what you sense with what you do, in a way that handles noise, delays, and uncertainty. The better your perception, the more confident your control can be, and the safer your robot becomes.

One practical approach is sensor fusion. No single sensor gives a perfect picture all the time. Cameras see colors and shapes but miss depth; lidar or radar gives distance but not texture. When you combine sensors, you get a more reliable view. Think of a line-following robot that uses a camera to see the line and a small gyro to know how the robot is tilted. By fusing these cues, you can decide not just where you are on the line, but whether you are skidding or slipping, and you can compensate more quickly.

Two fundamental ideas here matter most. First, state estimation—keeping a trusted estimate of the robot's position and motion despite imperfect measurements. Filtering methods, like simple low-pass filters or more advanced Kalman filters, help separate real motion from sensor noise. Second, robust control—designing the controller to tolerate modest errors and delays. You don't have to be perfect to be effective; you just need to be predictable and safe.

Two short scenarios illustrate how perception and control come together. Scenario A: A robot vacuum cleans a room with furniture. It uses bump sensors, infrared meters, and a camera to estimate where it is relative to walls and open space. The controller then decides how fast to move and where to turn, adjusting on the fly when it detects a chair leg or a door threshold. Scenario B: A small drone flies inside a warehouse. It reads obstacles with a forward-facing camera and depth sensor, estimates wind gusts and drift with a lightweight filter, and uses predictive control to plan a smooth path that avoids shelves while keeping a steady flight.

Three steps to fuse perception and control in your design:

Step 1: Pick a simple fusion strategy. Start with a small combo of sensors and a straightforward filter to combine their readings. Rationale: A simple blend is easier to understand and tune, and you'll see immediately how perception affects motion.

Step 2: Tie perception to the control signal directly. Use the fused estimate to set the error input for your controller. Rationale: When perception informs the error, corrections reflect the real world more accurately.

Step 3: Test under realistic disturbances. Add noise, delays, or moving obstacles and watch how the system copes. Rationale: Realistic tests reveal weaknesses you can address before production.

Two more micro-cases help connect concepts. Micro-case 1 shows a warehouse robot using a fused estimate of its own pose and obstacle locations to plan a safe path with MPC. The robot respects speed limits, stays at a safe distance from other robots, and slows gracefully when a person steps into its lane. Micro-case 2 demonstrates a home assistant robot that uses perception fusion to detect stairs and avoid a fall. It adapts its motion to the stairs' edge, improving safety without sacrificing task completion speed.

Exercises

1) Open-loop vs closed-loop demonstration (10–15 minutes). Build a tiny test where you drive a small wheeled robot through a simple track with and without feedback. Measure how closely the robot follows the track in each case and note the difference in control effort.

2) PID tuning sprint (15–20 minutes). Use a line-following bot on a straight line. Start with

small gains, then adjust Kp, Ki, and Kd to minimize deviation. Record the maximum deviation and the time to regain the line after a small disturbance.

3) Perception-to-control test (20–25 minutes). Use a simple sensor setup (camera or distance sensor plus a basic filter). Build a short routine where the perception readings feed the control input to keep an object at a target distance. Measure response time and steady-state error.

4) Quick MPC thought exercise (15 minutes). Sketch a tiny map of a track with obstacles. Draw a horizon and a few potential future steps. Describe in words how an MPC planner would choose the first action to stay safe and on course.

Troubleshooting

- If your robot oscillates a lot with a PID controller, reduce the proportional gain first, then sparsely adjust the derivative term to dampen the motion. If it continues to oscillate, check sensor timing and ensure the error measurement is stable. A noisy error signal often causes erratic motion.

- If the robot is slow to react or never reaches the target, gently increase the proportional gain, but monitor for overshoot. If overshoot appears, introduce a small derivative term or a tiny amount of integral to correct steady drift without reintroducing large swings.

- If you switch to an MPC or adaptive method and computation becomes a bottleneck, trim the horizon or simplify the model. Too heavy a model can slow decisions enough to create unsafe behavior.

- If perception seems laggy or unreliable, verify sensor calibration and data rates, and try a lightweight filter to reduce noise before feeding the controller. A smoother input often yields calmer motion.

- If the robot misreads obstacles and edges, add a safety margin in your planning and check for sensor fusion consistency. A conservative bias can prevent many unsafe events.

Tools and templates

- PID tuning quick template: Start with Kp near a small value, Ki and Kd near zero. Incrementally adjust Kp, then Ki, then Kd, and log the resulting behavior. Use a simple table to track changes and outcomes (Kp, Ki, Kd, observed behavior, time to settle).

- MPC planning quick sheet: Define the robot's model in a few lines (how fast it moves in a straight line, how it turns), set a horizon (short for beginners), note constraints (speed, turning radius), and record the first action chosen by the planner for a few example scenarios.

- Perception-to-control checklist: 1) Verify sensor data rates; 2) Confirm filter outputs are stable; 3) Check that the control input responds smoothly to perception changes; 4) Test with a modest disturbance and record recovery time.

Key Takeaway: Small, deliberate feedback and thoughtful planning unlock reliable navigation; start simple, then add layers of smart control as you gain confidence.

Transition: In the next chapter, you'll learn how robots move their arms and grab things. Coming up next Subtittle: Robot Manipulation and Grasping

1) Forward and inverse kinematics for manipulators,

2) Grasp planning, end-effector design, and force/torque sensing,

3) Planning and executing manipulation in cluttered, dynamic scenes

Chapter 7

Robot Manipulation and Grasping

Forward and inverse kinematics let you move a robotic arm exactly where you want, grab objects with the right grip, and plan actions even when scenes get messy.

Forward kinematics for manipulators

You start by looking at the arm as a chain of links connected by joints. Each joint changes the shape of the chain, and the goal of forward kinematics is simple: if you know every joint angle or displacement, you can calculate exactly where the end of the arm—the hand or gripper—will be in space. This step tells you the position and orientation of the end-effector from the robot's own internal settings.

Think of a basic two-link arm with two rotating joints. If the first joint angle is a degrees and the second is b degrees, and the links have lengths L1 and L2, you can roughly picture the end as reaching out to a point defined by a couple of sine and cosine expressions. In more joints or three dimensions, the math gets longer, but the idea stays the same: each joint adds a layer of rotation or displacement, and you combine them to map from joint space to Cartesian space.

Why this matters: knowing the exact end position lets you plan where you want the hand to go before you move anything. It also helps you simulate what would happen if you turn a few joints a certain way, without actually moving the real arm.

Inverse kinematics for manipulators

Inverse kinematics asks the opposite question: given a desired end-effector pose (where you want the hand to be and how it should be oriented), what joint angles or displacements will get you there?

This is how you translate a target position into real motor commands.

In simple arms with a couple of joints, you can often solve inverse kinematics with closed-form formulas. In more complex arms, especially those with many joints or in three-dimensional space, you usually use numerical methods. You might start with an initial guess and iteratively adjust the joints until the end-effector sits at the target pose. Sometimes there are multiple valid solutions, and sometimes there's no exact solution due to joint limits or obstacles. When that happens, you set tolerances and find the closest feasible pose.

A few practical notes

- Singularities are tricky moments where small joint moves cause large end-effector moves, or where movement possibilities collapse. You handle them by changing the approach—slightly adjusting another joint, or choosing a nearby feasible pose.

- Redundancy is common: robots often have more joints than strictly needed to reach a pose. You can use this extra freedom to avoid obstacles or to keep joints in safer, more comfortable ranges.

- Real robots mix forward and inverse kinematics with sensing. If sensors show the arm is not where it should be, you correct in real time.

A micro-case to see the ideas in action

Case A: a simple planar arm with two rotary joints reaches for a cube on a table. L1 and L2 are equal to a known length, and the target is directly in front of the shoulder. By applying the inverse kinematics, you compute two possible elbow angles that place the hand at the cube's center. You pick the solution that keeps the elbow in a comfortable position and avoids colliding with the table edge. You then verify the motion with a quick forward kinematics check before moving.

Case B: a three-joint arm reaches for a cup on a shelf. You first compute a rough IK to point the hand toward the cup, then adjust the wrist orientation to match the cup's opening. If the shelf has other objects nearby, you treat those as obstacles and plan a path that avoids them while still placing the gripper at the target pose.

Grasp planning, end-effector design, and force/torque sensing

Grasp planning is all about choosing how the hand or gripper should touch the object to hold it securely. End-effector design means picking or shaping the tool that will grip, press, squeeze, or lift. Force and torque sensing give you feedback about how the grip feels, so you can adjust pressure in real time.

End-effector design choices

- Grippers: A two-finger or three-finger hand can pinch, cradle, or wrap around objects. The geometry matters: flat fingers prefer flat surfaces, rounded fingers help with small or irregular shapes.

- Suction grippers: A suction cup can grab flat, smooth surfaces quickly, but the object must be compatible with a strong seal.

- Hybrid or specialized tools: Some tasks need both gripping and pinching modes or an integrated sensor suite to measure contact pressure.

Grasp planning basics

- Stability matters: a stable grasp resists slipping as you lift or move the object. The grasp should balance friction, contact area, and the object's shape.

- Pre-grasp and grasp planning: you first estimate a good approach, then reach and close the fingers around the object. If you can, plan a contact strategy that sets up the hand for a secure lift right away.

- Tactile and force feedback: sensors tell you how hard the fingers press and where contact occurs. If the grip starts to slip, you can tighten slightly, adjust the contact points, or re-plan the approach.

End-effector design in practice

You choose the design to fit the task. If you handle many small items, smaller fingers with precise motion help. If you lift oddly shaped blocks, broader fingers or compliant material reduce slipping. An effective end-effector design combines shape, stiffness, and sensing so you can feel the object and respond to changes during a lift.

Force/torque sensing and feedback

Touch matters. Force sensors tell you when to increase or decrease grip force, and torque sensing helps detect awkward twists or off-axis loads that could drop the item. This feedback loop is essential when you pick uncertain objects or work near fragile items. In a safe routine, you keep latency low so your system can react quickly if grip changes.

A practical illustration

Imagine a two-finger gripper picking up a small block. You plan an approach angle that places the block near the center of the gripper. The fingers close with a gentle squeeze, and force sensors confirm the block's contact points form a stable grip. If the reading shows the block starting to tilt, you slightly adjust finger positions and reapply a balanced grip. The end result is a solid hold without crushing the item or losing grip during movement.

Planning and executing manipulation in cluttered, dynamic scenes

Cluttered and dynamic scenes add complexity. Objects sit close together, light changes, and people or robots move around. You need a plan that can adapt and keep the task moving.

Perception and environment understanding

First, detect where objects sit and how they're oriented. Use simple cues like edges, shapes, and color to identify potential targets. Then build a mental map of nearby obstacles, including walls, shelves, and other arms. In dynamic scenes, you keep an eye on moving objects and adjust your plan as needed.

Motion planning with safety buffers

You map a path from start to end that avoids collisions. When space is tight, you use smaller, incremental steps and keep a safety margin. If the environment changes—say a person steps into the path—you pause, re-scan, and replan a safe route.

Grasp planning in clutter

Grasping in clutter means choosing contact points that also keep the object away from other items. You may plan a sequence: approach, approach again from a slightly different angle if the first path is blocked, grasp, and lift. If there's another object nearby, you consider how lifting one item affects the others and adjust accordingly.

Dynamic re-planning and feedback loops

When things move, you need to re-check. You continuously compare what you planned with what you see. If there's a mismatch, you replan on the fly, perhaps choosing a new approach, a different grasp, or an alternate path to the goal. The system's ability to adapt is often the difference between a successful pick and a dropped object.

Two quick micro-cases

Case C: An arm must grab a can on a moving conveyor belt. The target is never still. You plan a grab that is robust to small shifts, use real-time vision to refine the hand's position, and rely on force feedback to ensure the can stays secure as it lifts and transfers.

Case D: A robot needs to retrieve a book from a crowded shelf. The scene is tight; nearby items risk being nudged. You approach from a clear angle, contest a stable grip, and slowly lift while watching for any contact changes that might indicate a shift in balance. If the shelf's arrangement changes, you pause and re-scan before continuing.

Exercises

1) Try a simple forward-kinematics check: sketch a two-link arm, assign lengths, pick two joint angles, and estimate the end-effector position.

Then compare to a quick hand calculation or a mental estimate of where the hand should be. Do this for two different angles. Time: 10 minutes. Measure progress by the closeness of your estimate to the computed position.

2) Design a basic end-effector idea and a pretend grasp: draw or describe a two-finger gripper that could hold a small block. Describe contact points, how the fingers would close, and how you would sense success with a simple force reading. Time: 15 minutes. Measure progress by how clearly you can explain the grasp and the sensing plan.

3) Plan a cluttered-pick scenario: picture a small object on a table among several nearby items. Write down a quick three-step plan: approach, grasp, lift. Add a safety margin to your path and describe how you would adjust if a nearby object shifted. Time: 20 minutes. Measure progress by the coherence and feasibility of the plan.

4) Quick troubleshooting exercise: imagine your IK result would place the hand in a position that collides with a nearby object. List two adjustments you could try to reach the target pose without collision. Time: 10 minutes. Measure progress by the ability to propose feasible alternative poses.

Troubleshooting

- IK has multiple solutions or none: choose the solution with joints staying within safe ranges and avoid awkward postures; if none works, slightly alter the end pose or adjust tolerances.

- Singularities cause unexpected motion: switch to a nearby pose that yields a stable configuration; if possible, use redundancy to bypass the singular position.

- Grasp slips or crushes the object: check grip force, re-check contact points, and re-plan with a more stable approach; use force feedback to fine-tune pressure.

- Obstacle or clutter blocks the intended path: re-scan, replan a different approach, or temporarily reposition the object if allowed.

- Dynamic changes complicate planning: re-run perception, update your map, and replan the motion with real-time feedback.

Templates and tools you can copy

- Kinematics setup template

Robot: a chain of links L1, L2, ..., with joints J1, J2, ... Jn

Each link length, joint type (rotary or linear), and joint limits

End-effector: type, grip surface, and sensing options

Key equations: forward kinematics to get end pose from joint values; inverse kinematics approach notes for target pose

- Grasp planning checklist

Object pose (position and orientation)

End-effector pose (grip surface alignment)

Contact points and expected friction

Grasp stability assessment and force/torque sensing plan

Safety margins and collision checks

- Movement and perception template

Perception inputs used (camera, tactile, force sensors)

Obstacles map and clearance distances

Planned path with steps and replan triggers

Acceptable end conditions and success criteria

Key Takeaway: Forward and inverse kinematics let you predict and reach any target pose, while grasp planning, end-effector design, and force sensing build reliable, gentle grips even in messy spaces.

Coming up next: Subtittle: Machine Learning and Reinforcement Learning in Robotics

1) Supervised and unsupervised learning for perception and prediction,

2) Reinforcement learning concepts, reward shaping, and policies,

3) Sim-to-real transfer, domain randomization, and sample efficiency

Chapter 8

Machine Learning and Reinforcement Learning in Robotics

By the end of this chapter, you will learn how machines in robots learn from data to see, predict, and decide, and how to move ideas from pretend worlds into real-world actions.

1) Supervised and unsupervised learning for perception and prediction

You use two big families of learning to help a robot understand its world: supervised learning and unsupervised learning. Supervised learning relies on labeled examples. You show the robot many pictures or sensor readings, and you tell it what each one represents—like "door," "wall," or "car." The robot looks for patterns that link the data to the labels, so when it sees new data later, it can guess the correct category. Unsupervised learning, on the other hand, does not need labels. The robot looks for structure on its own, grouping similar data together, spotting patterns, or reducing your data to a simpler form that still preserves the important ideas.

Step 1: Gather data with clear labels or recognizable structure. You collect examples from the robot's sensors—camera images, depth readings, or sound—and tag what matters in each case. The goal is to capture enough variety so the robot can tell real situations apart, like different types of surfaces, objects, or scenes. If you're using supervised learning, you'll need enough labeled data to cover common situations the robot will meet. If you're leaning on unsupervised learning, you'll look for natural groupings in the data, such as similar lighting, textures, or motion patterns.

Rationale: Good data is the seed of good learning. Labels steer the model toward correct answers, while unsupervised methods reveal hidden structure that you might not have labeled in advance.

Step 2: Choose your learning approach based on the data you collected. If you have strong, reliable labels for the tasks you care about (like obstacle types in a warehouse), use supervised learning to train a perception system that recognizes those obstacles quickly and accurately. If you don't have labels for every situation, or you want the robot to discover new patterns on its own, try unsupervised learning to group similar scenes or to learn compact representations of sensor data.

Rationale: The best choice depends on the data. Supervised methods can be extremely precise but need good labels; unsupervised methods can discover useful structure but may need extra steps to make that structure useful for a task.

Step 3: Train, validate, and monitor performance in a real or simulated world. You split your data into training and testing sets, tune choices like model size and learning rate, and check how well the model does on things it hasn't seen before. In the real world, you monitor the robot's predictions and observe when things go wrong, ready to retrain if the environment changes. You keep an eye on speed and resource usage so the system can run in real time on the robot's computer.

Rationale: Ongoing evaluation prevents surprises after you deploy. Real environments differ from the lab, and models can drift when lighting, weather, or backgrounds shift.

Micro-case 1: A delivery robot learns to distinguish doors from walls using supervised learning. You collect thousands of camera images from its routes, label each image as door or non-door, and train a fast detector. After testing, the robot can tell a doorway from a plain wall in diverse lighting with a reliable response time, helping it plan safe paths through hallways and rooms.

Micro-case 2: A service robot uses unsupervised learning to explore a new building and cluster its sensor data into "types of spaces." It doesn't start with labels for every room type, but it learns that crowded, bright spaces behave differently in the sensors than quiet, dim ones. Later, you can attach useful labels to those clusters to guide navigation and interaction without labeling every scene in advance.

2) Reinforcement learning concepts, reward shaping, and policies

Reinforcement learning (RL) is a way for robots to learn by trying actions and seeing what happens. Instead of teaching a robot every rule, you give it a goal and let it discover which actions bring the best results over time. The robot's brain, called a policy, maps situations to actions. Rewards are signals that tell the robot when its choices move toward the goal. You can shape rewards to encourage not just the fastest path, but also safety, efficiency, and reliability.

Step 4: Frame a problem as an RL task. You define a goal for the robot, describe useful surrounding states, and decide how the robot's actions affect the world. The key idea is that the robot learns by trial and error, gradually discovering which sequences of moves bring it closer to the goal. You also set up a way to measure what "good" looks like in this task, such as reaching a destination, avoiding collisions, or using less energy.

Rationale: Framing matters. A clear RL setup helps the robot understand when it is making progress and when it is failing, guiding it toward better strategies over time.

Step 5: Design rewards and policies with care. Rewards should reflect the task's real priorities: safety, speed, energy efficiency, or smoothness of motion. You can give small rewards for useful mid-step behaviors (like maintaining a safe distance from obstacles) and larger rewards for completing the goal. Policies describe what to do in different situations. You can start with simple strategies and let the robot improve them as it gathers experience.

Rationale: Thoughtful rewards steer learning. Poorly chosen rewards can teach the robot to game the system or ignore important details.

Step 6: Train in a safe, controlled environment and evaluate progress. Use simulations to let the robot practice a lot without risk, then test in real-world settings carefully. Watch for issues like overfitting to the simulation, which can make the robot perform poorly in the real world. If the robot struggles with rare or hard scenarios, you might introduce those as additional training examples or adjust the rewards to emphasize handling them.

Rationale: Realistic practice helps the robot gain robust skills. Balanced evaluation prevents chasing a narrow set of outcomes while ignoring others that matter in practice.

Micro-case 3: A small robot learns to navigate a maze using RL. The task rewards it for reaching the end and punishes it for hitting walls. In simulation, it tries thousands of routes, gradually discovering a policy that avoids dead ends and finds the fastest route without colliding. When moved to a real test track, it performs well enough to complete the maze reliably, showing how a learning policy can transfer from pretend to real-world play.

3) Sim-to-real transfer, domain randomization, and sample efficiency

Sim-to-real transfer is about moving what you learn in a virtual world to a real robot. The challenge is that simulated physics, lighting, textures, and noise aren't exactly the same as the real world. Domain randomization helps bridge that gap by deliberately varying those differences during training. The idea is simple: if the robot learns to handle a wide range of variations in simulation, it's more likely to cope with real-world variability after deployment. You also care about sample efficiency—how quickly the robot learns from data. Efficient learning means less time in training and faster deployment.

Step 7: Use simulation to prototype and test ideas before touching real hardware. You build a virtual version of your robot and its environment, run experiments, and compare outcomes. The aim is to explore many options quickly, find promising strategies, and weed out poor ones before you risk real-world hardware or people.

Rationale: Simulation is a safe testing ground. It saves time and reduces risk while you identify viable approaches.

Step 8: Apply domain randomization to narrow the sim-to-real gap. In their training, you randomize factors such as object positions, lighting, textures, and even sensor noise. The robot learns to cope with a wide range of appearances and sensor quirks, so when it faces the real world, it isn't surprised by small changes. This approach helps prevent a model from failing just because one detail in the simulation didn't match reality.

Rationale: Real-world variation can break a model that trained in a fixed simulation. Randomization teaches resilience by exposing the robot to many possible worlds.

Step 9: Watch for sample efficiency and plan careful deployment. If learning takes too long, you adjust the setup to be more data-efficient: better model architectures, smarter exploration strategies, or additional simulated experiences. When you transition to the real robot, you run cautious experiments, collect performance data, and iterate. You aim for a balance between speed of learning and reliability in real use.

Rationale: Practical learning means not overdoing data collection or training time. Efficiency helps you move from idea to real capability faster.

Micro-case 4: A robot arm learns a pick-and-place task in simulation with domain randomization. It experiences many different object sizes, textures, and positions, so its policy becomes robust. When you move to the real arm, it transfers the learned behavior with only modest adjustments, performing the task smoothly and accurately in a cluttered workspace.

Key Takeaway: Learning in robots comes in two flavors—teaching with labeled examples and guiding through trial-and-error—so you can build perception, plan actions, and adapt to new worlds by design, not by chance.

Coming up next Subtittle: Multi-Robot Systems and Coordination

1) Communication models and decentralized vs centralized control,

2) Task allocation, cooperative mapping, and formation strategies,

3) Scalability, fault tolerance, and multi-agent collision avoidance

Chapter 9

Multi-Robot Systems and Coordination

You will learn how to make a team of robots work together smoothly, sharing tasks, avoiding collisions, and staying scalable as the team grows.

Step 1. Decide how your team talks: centralized or decentralized control. In a centralized setup, one leader or a base station makes most decisions, and the others follow. In a decentralized setup, each robot talks to its neighbors and makes many choices on its own. Centralized control can be simpler to start with when the team is small, because there is a single place to plan and monitor everything. Decentralized control usually scales better, because there is no single bottleneck, and the team can keep working if one robot has trouble. The choice affects how you design messages, timing, and failure handling. A small warehouse team might use a central controller to guide movements, while a fleet of search robots in a large park might rely on neighbor-to-neighbor communication to keep moving when a link to the base is weak.

Step 2. Decide what information you will share and how often. Common essentials include where each robot is (its position), what task it is pursuing, and any changes to its plan or its local map. Some teams share only essential data to save bandwidth; others broadcast more detail to improve coordination. The key is to keep information accurate, timely, and not overwhelming. If messages get overwhelmed, robots slow down or misread signals, which can waste time or cause confusion. In practice, you can start with simple status updates every few seconds and map changes every minute, then adjust as you see how the team performs in real world or simulated tests.

Step 3. Set a simple rule for who talks when. You can use time-based schedules, event-based alerts, or a mix. For a small, centralized system, it helps to have a regular "check-in" cycle so every robot knows when to listen for orders and when to report. In a decentralized system, you can use local rounds where neighboring robots share updates before making a joint move. The goal is to avoid message collisions and to keep the flow predictable. A practical approach is to assign a clear order: announce critical changes first, then share routine status, and finally broadcast any new plans. This keeps the chatter productive and easy to follow.

Step 4. Pick a task allocation method that fits your team size and mission. Simple teams can use fixed roles, where each robot has a known specialty. Bigger teams can use auctions or market-based assignment, where robots bid for tasks based on current load or capability. The advantage of auctions is fairness and responsiveness; the downside is extra messaging and a little delay while bids are exchanged. A practical example: in a warehouse, one robot might specialize in high shelves, another in floor delivery, and a third in scanning. If a new item arrives, the closest capable robot can bid to take the task. This reduces travel time and balances workload automatically as the fleet grows.

Step 5. Coordinate shared maps and goals so the team stays on the same page. If robots rely on shared mapping, they must decide how often to share updates and how to fuse different local maps into one coherent picture. A simple rule works well: when a robot updates a critical part of the map (like the location of a new obstacle), it broadcasts that change and others adjust their plans. In cooperative mapping, each robot adds its local observations, and the group averages or consensus-fuses them to reduce errors. Clear protocols for map ownership, update timing, and conflict resolution help prevent every robot from trying to rewrite the same area at once.

Step 6. Design formation or streaming strategies that match the mission. Formations are patterns of movement that help coverage, safety, and efficiency. A line or column formation is common for moving through narrow aisles; a staggered or wedge formation can optimize sensing and redundancy in open space. You can also adopt a flexible slipstream: robots follow each other with safe spacing and adapt as the front robot changes direction. The main idea is to keep trajectories predictable and avoid crowding, so sensors don't confuse passes with obstacles. In practice, you may enforce a minimum gap and use simple relative positioning to maintain spacing even if the team reconfigures on the fly.

Step 7. Build for scalability so the team can grow without breaking coordination. Start with modular software that lets you add robots without rewriting the whole system. Use clear interfaces for communication, data formats, and task descriptions. Decentralized ideas often scale better because each robot only talks to its neighbors, yet you still need a way to share a general world view. You should plan for variable message loads, so the system remains responsive as the number of robots expands. Think about storage, bandwidth, and computation: keep critical decisions lightweight and let nonessential data ride along as optional updates. When you design for scalability, you're building a foundation that supports bigger missions later.

Step 8. Add fault tolerance so a single problem doesn't crash the whole mission. Expect hardware twists, weather changes, or temporary link losses. A robust team can continue operating even if one robot drops out or temporarily loses contact. Techniques include redundancy (backup paths for key tasks), health checks (regularly confirming that robots can still sense, move, and communicate), and graceful degradation (if a robot fails, others pick up its tasks without panic). You'll also want simple recovery rules: if a robot cannot complete a task, it hands it off to a nearby teammate with minimal delay. Practically, this means designing your system so it can re-route plans quickly and re-balance loads without human intervention.

Step 9. Put collision avoidance into the mix so your team can work safely and efficiently. This means both planning and sensing play a role. Early on, keep trajectories simple and separated by safe margins. As robots move, they reassess and adjust if someone else's path encroaches. Use conservative timing windows and local retry rules: if a planned move looks risky, slow down or pause until the path is clear. Coordination helps here, too: robots share intention estimates so no one surprises another with a sudden turn. In practice, combining reactive sensing with predictive planning reduces the chance of near-misses and keeps the fleet moving toward its goal.

Examples and micro-cases to see the ideas in action.

- Example one: In a campus delivery scenario, a small fleet uses a centralized controller to assign tasks based on proximity. When a courier request drops in, the controller assigns it to the best-suited robot, then broadcasts the plan. The chosen robot navigates, while others adjust their routes to avoid bottlenecks, keeping the flow smooth even as people move around.

- Example two: In a search-and-rescue drill in a damaged building, robots pair up in a decentralized setup. Each pair shares local maps with neighbors and negotiates who goes into tighter spaces. If one robot loses a link, its partner helps reroute tasks and maintains the group’s coverage, showing how resilience comes from local decisions guided by shared goals.

Exercises

1) Centralized vs decentralized practice (15–20 minutes). Set up a simple mock mission where one robot sends updates to a base station that then guides two other robots. Track how long it takes to complete a task and note any delays caused by communication. Measure how many messages are exchanged and whether all robots finish the task without conflicts. Reflect on which setup felt smoother and why.

2) Task allocation and mapping drill (20–25 minutes). Create a small test where four robots must assign four tasks. Try fixed roles first, then run

a simple auction-based allocation. Compare the time to allocate and the distance traveled by each robot. Observe how different methods handle a late-arriving task and what happens if one robot becomes unavailable.

3) Fault tolerance and collision avoidance test (15–20 minutes). Simulate a robot failure in the middle of a task. See how others reallocate its duties and adjust trajectories. Then introduce a near-collision scenario and practice reactive avoidance. Note how quickly the system recovers, and whether safe gaps are maintained throughout the exercise.

Troubleshooting notes

- Problem: Messages pile up and slow the team. Fix: simplify data; send only essential updates; stagger broadcasts to avoid jams.

- Problem: One robot consistently blocks others' paths. Fix: enforce spacing rules and re-plan routes with a light priority system that prefers the front robot's plan.

- Problem: A robot loses contact and the team stalls. Fix: have a fallback plan where nearby robots continue their task with a conservative safe mode, while the lost robot re-connects or hands off tasks on return.

- Problem: Task allocation lags or fights over the same task. Fix: add a simple priority rule or brief timeout to prevent deadlock; if needed, reassign with a quick local decision rather than waiting for a global signal.

Tools and templates you can copy

- Communication plan template: a one-page guide listing the chosen model, what data is shared, how often, and how conflicts are resolved.

- Task allocation sketch: a simple flow for fixed roles or a basic auction-like protocol, with a short example of messages and responses.

- Map-sharing rule set: a straightforward protocol for when to broadcast map updates and how to fuse them into the local view.

- Formation policy sheet: guidance on preferred formations for common layouts (open space, corridors, shelves) and how robots adjust to drift or reconfiguration.

Key Takeaway: Clear, simple coordination rules—how you communicate, how you assign tasks, and how you stay safe—let a multi-robot team work together reliably as it grows.

Coming up next: Deployment, Safety, and the Future of Robotics

In the next chapter, you'll explore how teams are tested, validated, and integrated into real systems; you'll consider safety, privacy, and accountability;

and you'll glimpse directions like edge AI, cloud robotics, and stronger human-robot collaboration. You'll see how testing and ethics shape practical, responsible robotics, ensuring that the power of AI in robotics serves people well.

Chapter 10

Deployment, Safety, and the Future of Robotics

You will learn how to plan, test, and responsibly deploy robotic systems, while considering safety, ethics, and future directions like edge AI and cloud robotics.

1. Define deployment goals and success metrics

Start by stating what the robot must achieve in its real world setting. Write down the tasks it will perform, where it will operate, and who will use it. Then pick a few clear success measures. For a delivery robot, success might mean on-time deliveries within a certain accuracy, low error rates, and minimal downtime. For an educational robot, success could be student engagement, ease of use, and safety incidents per week. The goal is to create a shared target so every test and decision points toward a tangible outcome. Rationale: when you measure the right things, you can tell quickly if a change helps or hurts. Practical focus beats grand aims every time. Think about safety boundaries, too—where the robot can operate, what it should avoid, and how operators will interact with it. If you can't imagine a useful measurement, pause and define one before moving on.

2. Build a validation plan with a simulation-first approach

Plan to test ideas first in a safe, controlled environment, ideally in software simulations that mimic real scenes. Create a set of scenarios that cover normal use, edge cases, and potential faults. Then outline what success looks like in each scenario: the robot completes the task, detects a problem, or gracefully stops and alerts a human. Rationale: simulations let you push hard on design choices without risk to people or equipment. They also help you spot gaps before you touch real hardware. When you do move from the screen to the physical robot, you'll shorten the learning curve because you've already rehearsed the decision logic and timing. If a scenario fails in simulation, revise the policy or the control code and rerun the test until it passes. Keep a log of results so you can compare after future changes.

3. Create a continuous integration and deployment pipeline for robotics software

Set up an automated flow that checks every change you make, from code edits to configuration tweaks. At a minimum, run unit tests on individual modules, then move to integration tests where modules work together, and finally run end-to-end tests in a simulator. When possible, include hardware-in-the-loop tests to verify that software changes behave on real sensors and actuators. Rationale: a good CI/CD loop catches regressions early and keeps the robot predictable. It also creates a reproducible process so teammates can reproduce tests exactly. A simple pipeline might run the tests on every commit, build a fresh simulation environment, and report results to a shared dashboard. If tests fail, the system should halt automatic deployment and require a review step before proceeding.

4. Integrate safety checks and risk assessment into design

Add hazard analysis early: identify what could cause harm, where the robot could collide with objects or people, and how sensor failures might mislead it. Create a simple risk rating for each hazard and tie fixes to the rating—stronger safeguards for high-risk items, lighter measures for lower-risk ones. Rationale: safety isn't a final add-on; it should guide design choices from day one. Implement practical safeguards such as safe-speed limits, emergency stop mechanisms, obvious warning signals, and robust fault detection. If a sensor fails, the robot should slow down or stop and switch to a safe mode. Engage operators and potential bystanders in a quick safety review so you learn about real-world concerns you might miss in software alone.

5. Address ethical, legal, and societal considerations

Think about how people interact with the robot and who is responsible for its decisions. Consider privacy: does the robot collect video, audio, or location data? If so, how long is that data kept, who can access it, and for what purposes? Be transparent with users about what data is collected and why. Also consider accountability: who makes the call if the robot causes a problem—the operator, the programmer, the company, or the manufacturer? Rationale: technology is powerful, but people deserve clarity about how it affects their lives. If you can't answer a question about rights, safety, or responsibility, pause and clarify the policy with teammates or supervisors before continuing. This chapter supports responsible use, not clever shortcuts that push risk onto others.

6. Plan data governance and privacy practices

Treat data as a valuable asset that needs rules. Minimize data collection to what's necessary for the job, and set clear rules for storage, access, and retention. Use strong access controls so only authorized people can view sensitive information. When possible, remove identifying details from data used for development or testing. Rationale: data handling that respects privacy builds trust and reduces legal risk. You don't need to reveal every tiny detail to every user, but you should explain the basics of what is collected and how it is used. Keep logs of data-handling decisions and be ready to adjust practices as the robot's tasks evolve. If you must share data externally, ensure it is anonymized or aggregated in a way that protects individuals.

7. Explore future directions: edge AI, cloud robotics, and enhanced human-robot interaction

Edge AI means running intelligence directly on the robot's own computer, which reduces latency and helps keep control inside the machine. Cloud robotics uses remote computing power and data storage to extend what the robot can do, with the trade-off of needing network connectivity and careful data management. Enhanced human-robot interaction focuses on making collaboration with people smoother, safer, and more intuitive—think clearer feedback from the robot, predictable behavior, and better handoffs when a human needs to take over. Rationale: these directions aren't magic; they're tools to solve real limits, like speed, memory, or the ability to learn from many similar tasks. If you're curious about one path, design a small test: run a lightweight edge model on-device while keeping heavier processing in the cloud, and compare how they handle a live scenario. Or prototype a simple human-robot interface to gather quick feedback on clarity and safety. Each experiment teaches practical lessons you can apply to future projects.

Two micro-cases to illustrate the steps in action

Micro-case A: A classroom helper robot is deployed to fetch supplies. The team defines its success metric as "no more than two near-miss events per week" and "90% task completion within five minutes." They run simulations with crowded hallways, then set up a hardware-in-the-loop test in a mock classroom. They implement a safety stop if the robot detects nearby students moving unpredictably, and they publish a short ethics note about data use for maintenance requests. After a few weeks, the CI pipeline flags a frequent false alarm in a corner of the room; engineers adjust the sensor fusion settings, re-run the tests, and the false alarms drop. The team documents the privacy plan for video data and shares it with school staff, ensuring everyone understands when and why the robot collects information.

Micro-case B: A small warehouse robot helps sort items on a line. The deployment goals include 98% accuracy in sorting and a maintenance window of under one hour per week. They validate in a simulator with multiple item types, then test with a live demonstration in a controlled zone. They add a risk control: if the system detects uncertain item type, it pauses and asks a human operator for confirmation. The operation uses edge inference for quick decisions and cloud processing for more complex recognition tasks during off-peak hours. Data from the tests is anonymized and stored with strict access controls, and employees receive a short briefing about how the robot uses data to improve efficiency. The outcome is smoother performance and clearer responsibilities for everyone involved.

Exercises

Exercise 1: Deployment goals workshop. Take 20 minutes to write down three concrete goals for a robot in your setting, plus three success metrics for each goal. Review with a peer and adjust based on feedback. Measure progress by whether the goals and metrics are now visible on a shared board and in the project plan.

Exercise 2: Build a mini CI check. In 40 minutes, set up a simple automated test for a small software module that controls a sensor or actuator. Ensure the test runs automatically on every change and reports pass/fail clearly. Check progress by confirming the test passes on a fresh commit and that results appear in the dashboard.

Exercise 3: Privacy and safety quick review. In 15 minutes, outline a basic privacy sketch for your robot, including what data is collected, how long it's kept, who can access it, and how it is protected. Share the sketch with a peer and refine it. Measure progress by having a short written policy ready for review.

Troubleshooting

- Problem: Tests pass in simulation but fail on real hardware. Fix: Recheck sensor calibration, timing assumptions, and hardware-in-the-loop integration. Validate that the real sensor data streams match what the simulator expects, and tighten any assumptions about latency or processing power.

- Problem: The robot stops unexpectedly or remains inert after a change. Fix: Recheck safety thresholds and fault-detection logic; run a narrow, isolated test to see if a single component triggers the stop. Increase logging around the fault so you can identify the trigger without guessing.

- Problem: Privacy concerns arise from new data collection. Fix: Pause deployment, review data flows, minimize collection, and add a clear, user-facing explanation of why data is needed and how it is protected. Update the data-handling plan before proceeding.

Tools and templates

- Deployment Readiness Checklist: clear goals, success metrics, risk assessment status, test plan, CI/CD pipeline status, safety controls, and privacy measures.

- Ethics and Privacy Review Template: scope of data, purposes, retention periods, access controls, consent where required, and a quick risk rating.

- Data Handling Plan Template: data categories, storage location, access rights, retention, anonymization rules, and data deletion procedures.

- Simple Incident Report Template: what happened, when, who was affected, impact, corrective action, and preventive steps.

Key Takeaway: Planning with safety, ethics, and future tech in mind makes robotics clearer, safer, and easier to improve over time.

Transition: In the next chapter, you will dive into Sensors and Perception to understand how robots actually sense the world and turn signals into meaningful decisions.

Dear Reader,

Thank you for exploring this series focused on failures and the power of comeback stories. If you find value in these stories and believe in the importance of embracing setbacks as part of growth, we appreciate your support. Please consider sharing a positive review on the platform where you accessed this series.

Your feedback helps spread the message, inspiring more young readers to see challenges as opportunities and to believe in their potential. We understand that mistakes happen, and we thank you for your understanding.

www.ingramcontent.com/pod-product-compliance
Lightning Source LLC
LaVergne TN
LVHW022211200926
848481LV00006B/1923

* 9 7 9 8 2 9 5 5 3 5 5 2 9 *